Original title:
The Jokes of the Junipers

Author: Gideon Barrett
ISBN HARDBACK: 978-1-80567-360-6
ISBN PAPERBACK: 978-1-80567-659-1

Whispers of the Witty Trees

In the forest where laughter thrives,
Tall trees wear grins, oh how they jive!
With rustling leaves, a ticklish breeze,
They share their secrets, with giggles with ease.

A squirrel chuckles, fluffs up its tail,
As wise old oaks spin humorous tales.
The pines trade puns in the morning light,
Their bark is bright, a comical sight.

Laughter Beneath the Needles

Beneath the needles, shadows dance,
A chorus of chuckles, a chance to prance.
The ground squirrels jump with tiny glee,
While branches bow low, just to see.

A woodpecker knocks with a rhythmic beat,
Its comical drumming, a whimsical treat.
With every peck, the forest ignites,
A symphony of joy, in giggly delights.

Juniper's Mischievous Muse

Among the junipers, a jesters' crowd,
Their playful whispers, boisterous and loud.
They tell riddles wrapped in green,
Crafting humor, crisp and keen.

The breezy laughter spreads like wings,
As nature’s jesters, they share their flings.
With twisting branches, they strike a pose,
In the heart of the woods, where comedy flows.

Tales from the Twisting Branches

Twisting branches, where stories lie,
Each bend a punchline, oh so spry.
A nut falls down, a slippery slide,
While cackling critters run to hide.

A raccoon grins with mischief in view,
Sharing tall tales that might just be true.
The mossy logs chuckle, green and neat,
In this funny haven, life can’t be beat.

The Humor Hidden in Green

In a grove where branches bend,
Whispers of laughter never end.
Leaves chuckle in the morning light,
Spreading joy, a quirky sight.

Breezes tease the playful boughs,
Tickling trunks, oh what a rouse!
Nature giggles with each sway,
Turning somber into play.

Acorns drop with a silly plop,
Squirrels dance, they never stop.
While shadows wiggle on the ground,
In this folly, laughs abound.

With each rustle comes a jest,
Tree trunks wearing mossy vests.
The canopy is full of cheer,
Beneath the green, fun draws near.

Quips of the Botanical Spirits

Amidst the leaves, a whispers play,
Roots tell tales in their own way.
Each petal holds a secret grin,
Where nature's humor doth begin.

The daisies wink in the bright sun,
Laughing at clouds that like to run.
Tulips tilt with a lively air,
Joking with daisies everywhere.

Bamboo sways with a comical stance,
As willows join in the dance.
Every bud has a punchline pure,
In the garden, mirth is sure.

From petals soft to briars sharp,
Frolicking tunes like a harp.
In every bloom, a laugh you'll find,
Nature's laughter, never blind.

Secrets of the Swaying Spruces

Tall spruces chuckle in the breeze,
Bending low to share their tease.
With every sway, they spin a tale,
Of breezy spirits that laugh and hail.

Pinecones drop like playful pranks,
While shadows dance in leafy ranks.
Roots entwine in a merry twist,
In this forest, joy can't be missed.

Winds whisper jokes through the pine,
Tickling branches, oh how they shine.
The trunks rumble with a hearty cheer,
In this forest, laughter's near.

Each needle sways with wit so bright,
In the twilight, a charming sight.
Spruces laugh through day and night,
Nature's secrets, pure delight.

Echoes of Amusing Evergreen

In the grove where green trees stand,
Echoes of laughter fill the land.
Evergreens chuckle in the shade,
In playful games, the sun is played.

Branches sway with a jest so light,
As squirrels dance in pure delight.
Mossy carpets, soft and warm,
Invite whispers of nature's charm.

Beneath each bough, the shadows teem,
With giggles born from nature's dream.
In every flicker of the light,
The ever-joyful forest's sight.

Chirps and caws join the fun,
In this wood, joy is never done.
With each rustle, hilarity reigns,
In every tree, laughter remains.

The Playful Prankster of the Forest

In the shade where shadows dance,
A rascal spins a tale of chance.
With twigs and leaves, a crafty scheme,
The trees erupt with laughter's dream.

Behind the bark, the whispers gleam,
As squirrels join the playful theme.
The wind carries a giggling sound,
Through every nook and woodland ground.

Mischief makes the branches sway,
With every prank, they laugh and play.
A bouncing acorn, a strange delight,
Turns quiet dusk into pure light.

The forest bustles, full of cheer,
Where every prank brings friends near.
And in this merry, leafy court,
The humor thrives in nature's sport.

Sassy Sprouts in the Sunlight

Little sprouts with laughter bright,
Twist and twirl in morning light.
They share secrets of the breeze,
In giggles that shake the towering trees.

With petals wide and leaves all aglow,
They jest about the crowds below.
Each flower's quip, a burst of fun,
Sassy blooms just like a pun!

“Who wears green best?” they tease and poke,
Each stem a joke, each leaf a cloak.
In sunlight's dance, their laughter sings,
As nature bleeds the joy it brings.

Yet when the clouds begin to frown,
These silly sprouts will not back down.
They sway with glee, they know the score,
In every raindrop, they laugh some more.

Banter Beneath the Boughs

Underneath the leafy dome,
Chirpy birds call this place home.
Their chatter sparkles in the air,
Bantering jokes without a care.

"Did you hear the one about the tree?
It dropped a nut; oh how funny!"
With each chirp, they plot their fun,
Crafting laughs till day is done.

The foxes chuckle, rolling tight,
In a meadow, what a sight!
With winks and smirks, they join the game,
Nature's jesters, none the same.

And as dusk drapes a golden hue,
The laughter trails like morning dew.
A symphony of joy resounds,
In every corner, joy abounds.

Folly in the Forest's Embrace

Deep in the woods where shadows play,
Folly reigns, come what may.
Raccoons bandit with masks of sly,
Stealing snacks, oh me, oh my!

The wise owls share their quirky lore,
Joking about the forest floor.
“Who’s sneaking snacks?” they hoot with glee,
While fireflies giggle, bright and free.

In every rustle, a chuckle rides,
With playful tales that no one hides.
The trees conspire, the bushes grin,
A whimsical dance where joy begins.

So come and join this merry spree,
In forest’s arms, let spirits be.
With folly surged like sap in spring,
A chorus of laughter the woods will bring.

Laugh Lines in the Leaves

In a forest lush and bright,
The trees share laughs at night.
Squirrels giggle at the breeze,
Tickled by the rustling leaves.

Buzzing bees perform a dance,
With each twist, a silly chance.
Branches sway with glee and jest,
Nature's humor at its best.

Quips from the Quercus

Old oak stands, wise and bold,
Whispers tales of laughter untold.
Branches shake with merry cheer,
As woodland critters gather near.

Acorns drop from lofty heights,
Landing softly, funny sights.
Every thud a comic scene,
Nature's way of keeping keen.

Rib-Tickling Roots

Beneath the ground, roots intertwine,
Sharing secrets, oh so fine.
One says, 'Hey, we’re quite the pair!'
Another laughs, 'We’re rooted there!'

Worms tell tales of journeys wide,
With each wiggle, joy and pride.
In the soil, they find their groove,
Tickled by the laughter's move.

Comedies of the Conifer

Pines stand tall with needles high,
Tickling clouds that pass on by.
Each breeze brings a funny sound,
Echoes laugh from all around.

The cones drop down with comical flair,
Causing giggles from those who stare.
Sprightly shrubs chime in for fun,
A jestful show for everyone.

Rambunctious Roots

Beneath the earth, where pokers play,
Roots twist and turn in a silly display.
They tug on worms, all in good jest,
Making the soil a rip-roaring fest.

A squirrel drops acorns, they bounce and roll,
Roots chuckle softly, losing control.
What's this ruckus? The ground shakes wide,
Here comes a rabbit, it's rooted inside!

With glee they gossip, roots intertwine,
Sharing the punchlines of the ancient vine.
Each tickle of dirt, a giggle or two,
Laughter abounds where the wildflowers grew.

When breezes blow, they sway to the beat,
Roots dance together, oh, what a treat!
Out in the wild, they throw a grand bash,
In the roots' wild world, it's all about splash!

Joking with the Juniper Jumble

In the thicket where junipers play,
Berries laugh in the light of day.
They wiggle and jiggle, a sight to behold,
Spreading giggles in shades of gold.

With every sway, they tell a new tale,
Of cheeky critters and dandy snails.
Squirrels go cheeky, jump out with flair,
Junipers burst out, a giggly pair.

Their branches weave tales of pranks gone wrong,
Like owls who hooted at a busy throng.
Sunbeams peek in, casting shadows wide,
Makes the whole juniper forest feel spry.

Even the breeze gets swept in the fun,
Tickling leaves until the day's nearly done.
So if you wander to junipers bright,
Hear whispers of joy in the starry night!

The Sway of Silly Sprouts

Amidst the garden of giddy delights,
Sprouts sway and giggle under starry nights.
With petals that tickle and leaves that dance,
Each little sprout gets lost in a prance.

They swap funny tales of raindrop cheers,
And how they dodge bugs, invoking loud sneers.
One sprout shouts loudly, “Look at me twirl!”
As others roll over, their giggles unfurl.

A bumblebee buzzes, joins in their game,
Tickled by pollen, it adds to the fame.
Sprouts tell of suns and the laughter of skies,
With roots in the dirt, as they mimic the flies.

So if you wander where the sprouts take flight,
You’ll find tales of fun in the warm moonlight.
A frolicsome dance, where smiles abound,
In the sway of the sprouts, true joy can be found!

Cackles from the Canopy

High up in branches, the laughter resounds,
Cackles and chuckles, the forest astounds.
Where leaves twirl and play, in bright sunlight,
Canopies giggle till the sky turns night.

Birds tease the breezes with songs of delight,
Squirrels join in, creating a sight.
Each rustle a punchline, each branch a jest,
A forest full of fun, where humor is blessed.

The owls keep secrets, they wink with a grin,
Spreading their wisdom under thick, leafy skin.
Laughter echoes, a whimsical dance,
As sunlight plays tag, putting shadows in trance.

So visit the canopies, let your heart soar,
Where laughter can linger, and joy is galore.
In the trees, find giggles that make your heart leap,
For the cackles of nature are treasures to keep!

Nature's Playful Palette

In gardens where the daisies sway,
The bees wear ties to dance and play.
A squirrel juggles acorns with glee,
While flowers giggle in the tree.

The carrots tell a joke so grand,
A beet laughs hard, can't quite stand.
While sunflowers wink in the breeze,
Sharing secrets with the bees.

The butterflies wear silly hats,
As frogs tell tales to snickering cats.
A rainbow tickles the morning dew,
And the daisies blush in a charming hue.

In every nook, there's laughter bright,
Nature's canvas, pure delight.
So wander through this vibrant scene,
And find the humor in the green.

The Humor of the Herbaceous

In the herb patch, where laughter brews,
Thyme bakes cookies, surprising the blues.
Oregano sings with a raspy voice,
While basil joins in, making a choice.

The peppermint teases the chamomile,
With punchlines fresh, they share the meal.
A carrot plays the fool with flair,
Tickling radishes without a care.

The garlic grins with a pungent jest,
While lettuce smiles, feeling blessed.
Parsley winks, holding a bouquet,
In this garden theatre, all want to stay.

The herbaceous crew, in a joyful spree,
Crafting laughter, wild and free.
So join the fun in this leafy nook,
Where humor grows, just take a look.

Tales Told in Towhee Tones

In treetop realms, the towhees sing,
Whispers of humor in the spring.
With chestnuts roasted and stories spun,
They chirp and chuckle, having fun.

A worm tells tales of daring flights,
While sparrows blush with playful sights.
The crows crack jokes with cawing flair,
As the squirrels nod and hop in pair.

In each nest, there’s a punchline shared,
As nature’s critters have fun prepared.
With shadows dancing in the light,
The towhees' chorus brings pure delight.

Oh, sing along in the leafy glade,
With laughter and tunes, a grand parade.
Nature’s stage with wings aglow,
In every note, the joy will flow.

Lighthearted Lushness

In fields where wildflowers weave their lace,
They toss their petals, a giggly race.
Bumblebees buzz their bubbly song,
As they dance in the air, all day long.

Dandelions puff, playing tricks on the breeze,
Sending wishes with a mischievous tease.
While clovers chuckle in sunlit spots,
Whispering laughter and tying knots.

The grasses sway in a gentle jig,
With ladybugs clapping, oh how they dig!
While the sun winks, painting skies bright,
In this lush land, oh what a sight!

So frolic along with the merry crowd,
In nature's laughter, bright and loud.
For in every corner, joy does reside,
A world of whimsy where dreams collide.

Humor Hides in the Heights

Up in the branches, laughter swings,
Where every pinecone jester sings.
A squirrel drops acorns with flair,
And giggles echo through the air.

Laughter bubbles from creek to tree,
A chorus of glee, wild and free.
Branches bend with a playful tease,
As shadows dance in the warm breeze.

Nature's jesters, bold and spry,
Whisper secrets as they fly.
The sun winks down, a playful sprite,
In this forest of pure delight.

Whimsy from the Woods

Beneath tall trees, a riddle plays,
With critters plotting in silly ways.
A deer wears glasses, all askew,
While frogs in tuxedos croon a tune.

The mushrooms giggle, bright and round,
As shadows prance upon the ground.
An owl hoots jokes with wisdom's grace,
While moonbeams twirl in this funny place.

Rabbits bounce with a mischief's cheer,
While whispers of laughter draw us near.
In this woodland, joy unfolds,
With every story the forest holds.

Parodies of the Ponderosa

In tall pines where the rivers flow,
The wind tells tales of friend and foe.
A crow in a cape strikes a funny pose,
While turtles in crowns strike silly throes.

Bears in bow ties dance with glee,
Sipping on honey from the tallest tree.
Critters gather for a grand parade,
With laughter lighting every glade.

Jokes on the breeze when the sun is high,
As shadows stretch beneath the sky.
Laughter mingles with sweet perfume,
In this ponderous, playful room.

A Sylvan Spoonful of Laughter

In tranquil woods, where whispers play,
A spoonful of mirth brightens the day.
Squirrels trade jokes in a nutty jest,
While flowers chuckle in their colorful vest.

The brook babbles tales of silly sights,
Reflections dance in the soft moonlights.
Foxes in scarves twirl without shame,
In a wild game of chase, free from blame.

With every breeze, a giggle slips,
From the trees' embrace to the river's lips.
So join the fun on this joyous path,
Where laughter's the key, and play's the craft.

Teasing Tendrils of Time

In the breeze, the branches sway,
Tickling tales of yesterday.
Rustling leaves form giggles bright,
Whispers dance with pure delight.

Sunbeams wink from up above,
As shadows tease, they push and shove.
Nuts and pinecones drop in jest,
Nature's laughter, never rest.

Squirrels chatter, hopping 'round,
Chasing giggles off the ground.
Branches bow with silly grins,
As the woodland fun begins.

Time spins gently, soft and bold,
Every moment, a tale retold.
With cheeky charm, we sway in rhyme,
In the teasing tendrils of time.

Cheeky Conversations of the Canopy

Up above, the leaves are gabbing,
Swaying gently, laughter grabbing.
Branches shake with playful pride,
As birds join in, side by side.

Breezes burst with charming quips,
Creating mirth through whispered slips.
Every rustle, a hidden joke,
In the trees, their laughter woke.

Squirrels scurry, plotting fun,
Chased by shadows, on the run.
Clever critters, all a-flutter,
Playing pranks, what a clutter!

In the green, cheeky banter flows,
Among the boughs, a comedy show.
Nature's jesters, wild and free,
In conversations of canopy.

Whimsy Woven in Woodlands

In the heart of the woods, giggles bloom,
Whimsy weaves through every room.
Acorns tumble, dances start,
Nature's jest, a merry heart.

Tricky vines play hide and seek,
While branches sway and softly peak.
Frolicking fawns with prancing feet,
Join the jest with rhythmic beat.

Every shadow, a playful tease,
Calling all to join with ease.
Rustic paths with laughter trace,
Every step a joyous race.

Beneath the canopy, secrets hide,
Whimsy's charm can’t be denied.
In this woodlands, mirth takes flight,
Crafting joy, twinkling bright.

The Frivolity of Fragrant Foliage

Leaves whisper sweetly, scents arise,
Fragrant laughter fills the skies.
Petals giggle, colors plea,
In this dance, joy's decree.

Breezes tease, a fragrant jest,
Every bloom a vibrant fest.
Silly bees in playful throng,
Buzzing melodies, sweet and strong.

Twisting trunks share tales of cheer,
Every rustle brings us near.
The woodland scents with laughter blend,
As blooming joy knows no end.

Frivolous charms in nature's sway,
Invite us all to laugh and play.
In every scent, a joyous pledge,
Fragrant foliage on the edge.

Sylvan Shenanigans

In the woods where whispers play,
Trees dance and the breezes sway.
Squirrels chuckle in the sun,
Nature's laughter, pure and fun.

A rabbit hops with nimble grace,
Winking with a cheeky face.
Branches sway, and the leaves clap,
Joyful echoes on the map.

The mushrooms grin, all spry and bold,
Tales of mischief yet untold.
A chipmunk jests with acorn hats,
Witty remarks among the mats.

Brushing past the leafy cheer,
A songbird's chirp is bright and clear.
Laughter lingers, soft and sweet,
In this realm of giggles neat.

The Juniper's Jests

Underneath the green so bright,
Oddities bring pure delight.
The shadows flicker, play a tune,
Laughter swirls beneath the moon.

A hedgehog stumbles, rolls on by,
With a twinkle in his eye.
Old owl hoots a clever pun,
In the twilight, full of fun.

Whispers travel with the breeze,
Carried far among the trees.
Little critters share a grin,
In this comedy, we all win.

Twinkling stars join in the jest,
In this glade, we feel so blessed.
Echoes dance through boughs and leaves,
In these woods, we find reprieves.

A Comedy in the Canopy

High above where the wild things play,
Birds are gossiping all the day.
Laughter drips like warm spring rain,
From branches thick with joy and gain.

A bear attempts to climb a tree,
And tumbles down—oh, what a spree!
The raccoons cheer, they clap their paws,
Imagining their next big cause.

A fox with pranks up his furry sleeve,
Plots mischief, one may not believe.
Leaves rustle and a tale unfolds,
Filled with warmth, yet bold and cold.

The canopy sings with endless glee,
As shadows dance quite playfully.
All who wander lose their pain,
In this world where laughs are gain.

Chuckles Amongst the Needles

In a grove where needles gleam,
The sunbeams dance—a lively dream.
Jovial whispers tickle the air,
Nature's joy, an endless fair.

A porcupine tells a silly tale,
While butterflies flutter without fail.
Each chuckle floats on a gentle breeze,
Spreading merriment through the trees.

The leaves shimmy, the branches sway,
In this forest, fun leads the way.
Dancing shadows cast a spell,
Entwining laughter like a shell.

Underneath the velvet sky,
The critters grin, and spirits fly.
In every nook and friendly glade,
Joy blooms bright, never to fade.

Sprightly Sprigs of Humor

In the forest where shadows play,
Laughter dances through the day.
Leaves chuckle as breezes tease,
Nature's whimsy brings us ease.

Boughs bend low with merry glee,
Whispers of joy in every tree.
Squirrels giggle, the rabbits grin,
Life’s a jest, let the fun begin.

Mossy carpets hide some jokes,
Among the roots, the laughter pokes.
Branches sway with silly cheer,
Echoing fun for all to hear.

So come along, don’t be shy,
Join the chat with twinkle-eyed spry.
In this grove, the humor flows,
Like sunny rays, it surely glows.

The Puns That Sprout

Underneath the shady boughs,
Punny tales draw gasps and “wow!”
Leafy whispers share their jest,
Nature's humor is the best.

Frogs croak jokes near the stream,
While fireflies flicker, like a dream.
Every sprout has something to say,
Laughter blooms in green ballet.

From acorn caps to twiggy jokes,
The woods are full of playful folks.
Each slip of wind, a punchline clear,
Leaves laugh out loud as we draw near.

So gather ‘round, let spirits lift,
In the grove, we find our gift.
With every chuckle, hearts will shout,
What a joy, these puns that sprout!

Woodland Wit and Wisdom

In the heart of the woodland glade,
Wisdom grows in a funny shade.
With each breeze, a clever quip,
Nature's humor on a trip.

The owls nod with knowing eyes,
As sly foxes spread their lies.
Every rustle, a witty line,
Among the branches, joy does twine.

Squirrels share their nutty tales,
While chipmunks giggle through the trails.
In this forest, laughter streams,
Tickling hearts like playful dreams.

From petals soft to sturdy trees,
Every inch is filled with ease.
So let us roam where humor thrives,
In the woods, the spirit jives.

Echoes of Evergreen Laughter

In the shade of tall green pines,
Echoes float on playful lines.
Giggles bounce from branch to ground,
In this realm, joy does abound.

From the thicket, wisecracks sprout,
Silly antics dance about.
The brook chuckles with each glide,
As nature laughs and takes a ride.

Breezes carry glee and cheer,
All the woodland creatures near.
Every murmur hints at fun,
In the shades of setting sun.

So hike along this joyous path,
With laughter wide, forget the math.
For in the woods, where giggles play,
Life's a joke, come laugh away!

Chortles from the Clusters

In the boughs where laughter pricks,
Punny whispers dance and flicks.
Branches sway with every joke,
While the breezes giggle, poke.

Sunlight tickles every leaf,
Nature's jest is like a thief.
Stealing smiles from passersby,
As they chuckle, oh my, my!

Twisted trunks with great intent,
Share their tales, bizarrely bent.
Beneath them, wild fables grow,
Sprouting laughter row by row.

Buds burst forth with cheeky cheer,
Tickling ears of all who hear.
In this grove, light-hearted bliss,
Nature's humor, can't dismiss.

Wit Wreathed in Wood

Knotted roots and branches twist,
Crafting quirks that can’t be missed.
Swaying limbs share sly retorts,
As the forest plays its shorts.

Beetles laugh, the squirrels tease,
Echoes buzz upon the breeze.
With each rustle, jokes take flight,
In a canopy delight.

Sticks and stones become the rhyme,
Poking fun through space and time.
Every rustling leaf a sign,
That woodland whimsy is divine.

Old tree trunks hold secrets tight,
Wrapped in shadows, pure delight.
Nature's humor, rich and bold,
Wreathed in whispers, never old.

Guffaws in the Greenery

Amidst the leaves, giggles abound,
Where every inch of earth's renowned.
Bushes bow with hearty glee,
Sharing punchlines, wild and free.

Rabbits snicker, birds convey,
Comedic tales of their day.
Frogs croak out a ribbeting line,
Mixing fun with bubbles of brine.

Gnarled vines twist in jesting dance,
Inviting all to join the prance.
In this greenery, laughter sprawls,
Nature's theater, joyous calls.

Beneath the sun's embrace they play,
Every joke keeps gloom at bay.
In this grove, spirits ignite,
With guffaws that sound just right.

Anecdotes of the Arboreal

Stories whispered by the trees,
Tales that flutter on the breeze.
Branches croon of silly days,
In their own whimsical ways.

Leaves confide in grassy nooks,
Sharing laughs like cherished books.
Each note a spark, a wry remark,
While shadows dance, a lively lark.

Twisting trunks with glee adorn,
Patchwork humor—newly born.
Skits performed by stoic pines,
Line up well with playful signs.

Joy abounds in every bough,
Life's absurdity - take a bow!
In this green world, smiles extend,
As the arboreal wits transcend.

Frolics in the Forest Freestyle

In a glade where shadows play,
The squirrels dance in their ballet.
Trees chuckle in the dappled light,
While rabbits hop with sheer delight.

Mushrooms wear their caps so wise,
But who can tell their wondrous lies?
A fox slips by in search of fun,
Chasing tails beneath the sun.

A parrot speaks of daily gripes,
While toads croak out their silly types.
Each rustle, giggle, and surprise,
Makes each critter roll their eyes.

As night descends, the fireflies glow,
They flicker in a comic show.
When dawn arrives, they disappear,
But laughter lingers, crystal clear.

Mirth Among the Mossy Memories

Beneath the canopy of green,
Mossy tales are seldom seen.
A wise old owl with stories vast,
Recalls the pranks from ages past.

A raccoon with his mischief bold,
Gathers treasures, shiny gold.
He hides them all in clever spots,
Keeping secrets—all the knots.

The hedgehogs giggle, rolling round,
In a game where laughter's found.
As nature spins her merry tale,
Each creature joins, no chance to fail.

When stars peek out and shadows creep,
The forest hums, it’s time to leap.
For in this place, where fun’s the rule,
Mirth and magic truly fuel.

Breezes of Banter

A zephyr whispers, soft and light,
As trees convene for a lively night.
With rustling leaves, they share their quirks,
As laughter under moonlight lurks.

The pine trees sport their funny hats,
While chatting with the playful bats.
Each gust of wind brings giggles near,
A symphony for all to hear.

Nature’s humor runs so deep,
In every nook, there’s joy to reap.
So let’s embrace this wondrous cheer,
For life’s too short to shed a tear.

With every twirl and every leap,
The forest keeps its secrets neat.
And as we roam through this delight,
We find the jokes that spark the night.

Larky Leaves and Laughing Limbs

In forests thick with verdant cheer,
The branches sway, their voices clear.
“Why don’t you join the dance, my friend?”
A leafy limb does happily send.

With every rustle, laughter flows,
As nimble thoughts begin to pose.
What’s better than a playful spree?
When roots and branches feel so free.

A playful breeze, its whispers bold,
Delivers tales of riches told.
Each droplet of dew, a wink of fate,
Tells us love in leaves won't wait.

So romp, oh friends, 'neath stars and sun,
In laughter’s arms, we all are one.
Through larky leaves, we'll glide and sway,
Creating joy in every way.

Mischief in the Meadow

In the meadow where laughter sways,
Silly critters dance and play.
A rabbit wore a hat too wide,
As birds took turns to giggle and glide.

The daisies whispered jokes so bright,
While butterflies twirled in pure delight.
A squirrel cracked nuts with flair,
As all the flowers began to stare.

There's a pond that chuckles, oh so clear,
With frogs that croak without any fear.
The breeze carries laughter high,
As playful clouds drift in the sky.

At dusk, the fireflies start their light,
Winking at stars, bringing pure delight.
With mischief and cheer, the day does end,
In the meadow, there's giggles to send.

Giggles Under the Green

Beneath the branches, shadows dance,
Squirrels and acorns in a silly prance.
The leaves rustle with muffled glee,
As ants march by with a jolly decree.

A turtle wore shoes one size too small,
Tripping and tumbling, he had a ball.
The owls hooted with knowing winks,
While the brook bubbled, in playful blinks.

Laughter floats on the warm summer air,
As frogs ribbit jokes without a care.
The daisies nod, they cannot resist,
To join the fun, they sway and twist.

The sun dips low, the crickets sing,
As night wraps round like a cozy ring.
Under the green, joy takes a bow,
In this lively land, laughter's a vow.

Not So Serious Sprouts

Tiny sprouts peek from the ground,
With giggles and wiggles, joy is found.
Each little bud a prankster bold,
In shades of green, their stories told.

A flower dressed in polka dots,
Crackling with humor in garden plots.
The winds carry whispers of a pun,
As bees buzz by, joining the fun.

A chipmunk juggles berries with pride,
While a mischievous snail takes a ride.
The whole patch sparkles with mirth,
As laughter sprouts, filling the earth.

At twilight's laugh, the colors blend,
With stars above, the night extends.
Not so serious, these sprigs of cheer,
In every petal, laughter draws near.

The Playful Pinyon

Amongst the pinyons, laughter swells,
With tales spun of woodland spells.
A dancing pinecone rolls away,
As laughter echoes, night turns to day.

The critters gather in a giddy sprawl,
Swinging acorns and having a ball.
A chipmunk dressed in tiny gear,
Sings out a tune, all hearts to cheer.

A prankster wind steals hats from heads,
While giggles rise from all the beds.
The rustling leaves join in the jest,
In playful frames, they laugh the best.

As twilight wraps the playtime show,
The pinyons sway, put on a glow.
With every chuckle, the world spins round,
In the heart of the woods, joy is found.

The Jest of the Juniper Grove

In the grove, where shadows dance,
Junipers whisper, taking a chance.
A squirrel wears a tiny hat,
While a rabbit giggles, just like that.

The breeze carries laughter, soft and light,
As leaves play tag in the fading light.
A frog croaks jokes that make us cheer,
While wise old owls just wink and leer.

A hedgehog juggles acorns with glee,
While fireflies glow, a flickering spree.
The forest floor erupts in glee,
Nature's own jesters for all to see.

So gather round, as night unfolds,
In this grove where humor molds.
With every twist, there’s more to find,
In laughing woods, a jesting kind.

Woodland Whimsy in the Air

In the woods, a ticklish breeze,
Whispers through the dancing trees.
A rabbit hops with a goofy grin,
While badgers chuckle, thick and thin.

A porcupine tells tales so bold,
Of brave little bugs in armor of gold.
Branches sway, the trees take part,
In this merry dance that touches the heart.

Chipmunks form a chorus, sweet and neat,
While turtles tap their tiny feet.
Every leaf, a giggle shared,
In this woodland, all are compared.

Laughter rings, a joyful sound,
With every creature, fun is found.
In the air where whimsy flows,
Nature's jesters, as the twilight glows.

Chuckles of the Coniferous Clan

Beneath the pines, the jokes belong,
As squirrels scamper, singing their song.
A raccoon, masked, shares a few,
While wise old trees just chuckle, too.

The moonlight glimmers on the stream,
Where fish flash smiles, lost in a dream.
A deer cracks jokes, all soft and mild,
While the forest giggles, nature's wild child.

The stars above twinkle with glee,
Joining in the fun, wild and free.
Every rustle has a playful tone,
In this clan, no one feels alone.

As pine needles fall, laughter ignites,
Creating moments that feel so right.
Around the fire, they share their plan,
The nightly chuckles of the clan.

Sardonic Saplings at Dusk

As the sun dips low, shadows grow tall,
Saplings whisper secrets, one and all.
With wry little jokes in every sway,
Their laughter rings out at the end of the day.

A wise old willow joins in the fun,
Telling tall tales of how she outrun.
The breeze tickles each leaf and bud,
While maple trees wink, and the forest floods.

Chirping crickets write verses anew,
Creating a symphony only they knew.
Frogs croak sonnets, while owls conspire,
In this twilight theater, they never tire.

So listen close as the dusk unfurls,
In the land of saplings, where laughter swirls.
With every chuckle, the night takes flight,
In a world where humor turns wrong to right.

Jests in the Juniper Shadows

In the shade of the trees, laughter unfolds,
Whispers of secrets in green leaves told.
A squirrel plays tricks, a bird tries to sing,
Laughter resounds in the joy spring can bring.

A rabbit hops by with a curious stare,
Wishing for snacks but finds none to share.
The wind tells a tale, so silly yet sly,
Making the branches dance, oh so high.

Beneath the blue sky, all creatures agree,
Life's little mishaps make humor a spree.
With chortles and giggles, the forest's delight,
In juniper shadows, the world feels just right.

So come join the jest in this arboreal play,
Where laughter and joy make the worries decay.
The trees are the stage where the punchlines unwind,
In the jests of the junipers, fun's well-defined.

The Secret Life of Spruce

In the heart of the woods, spruce trees conspire,
Whispering jokes that could surely inspire.
A woodpecker knocks to add to the cheer,
While a fox laughs out loud at the antics he hears.

Down by the creek, a raccoon slips and falls,
Splashing the otters and echoing calls.
The salmon, they wiggle, with laughter so bright,
In the secretive forest, a surprising delight.

Among the green boughs, secrets take flight,
As squirrels share stories deep into the night.
A wise old owl chuckles from branches above,
The punchlines are plenty when covered in love.

Spruce trees keep secrets; their humor, the glue,
Binding together a world made anew.
For in this green haven, a giggle can grow,
Laughter rings out in the soft evening glow.

Amusing Antics of the Arbor

Within the tall trees, giggles take shape,
Frogs croak in chorus, old jokes reshape.
A deer steps lightly, then stumbles for fun,
As laughter erupts in the warmth of the sun.

The branches sway gently, a soft, playful tease,
Where shadows are playful and fill with such ease.
A bunny makes faces at passers nearby,
In the unkempt forest, the humor runs high.

A raccoon in mischief rolls down from a limb,
While a mischievous parrot performs his own whim.
They hop and they dance, making waves of pure glee,
In the arbor's embrace, so joyous and free.

So if you should wander where nature holds sway,
Look closely for laughter, it’s never far away.
The antics of trees, both clever and bright,
In the hearts of the branches, they’ll always ignite.

The Forest's Funny Bone

In the thickets and thorns, a jesting muse roams,
Each creature’s a joker, far away from their homes.
Squirrels with acorns, they play catch and throw,
Creating a racket, they put on a show.

A playful little badger digs tiny holes,
While chipmunks engage in their rib-tickling roles.
Laughter erupts as shadows collide,
In the forest's embrace where punchlines abide.

A turtle in slow-mo makes everyone grin,
As a rabbit hops past, with a wink and a spin.
The leaves whisper secrets of humor untold,
In the laughter of nature, bright memories unfold.

Here in the woods, where the funny bone lives,
Life offers a jest with the joy that it gives.
So come hear the giggles, they echo and hum,
In the heart of the forest, the laughter's a drum.

Jesting in the Juniper Grove

In the grove where shadows play,
The junipers dance in a quirky way.
One tells a tale, another a jest,
Leaves giggle softly, never at rest.

Critters chuckle, their laughter so bright,
As squirrels mimic, in morning light.
Breezes carry tales of mirth,
In this green haven, a place of worth.

When the sun dips low, a comedy show,
The branches sway as if they know.
A pinecone drops with a thud and a roll,
And laughter echoes, filling the shoal.

With every rustle, there's whimsy and glee,
Nature's own stand-up, for all to see.
Here in the grove, let worries take flight,
As jokes and joy fill the warm twilight.

Joviality of the Pines

Under pines, the stories ignite,
With playful banter, both day and night.
A branch bows down, as if to say,
"Come on, let's laugh, it's a fine day!"

The needles whisper, tales of old,
Of woodland frolics and treasures untold.
Woodpeckers tap a rhythm so sweet,
Joining in laughter, on nature's beat.

As shadows stretch, the moon winks bright,
Starlit giggles sparkle in flight.
With every twist and turn of the breeze,
Joy dances around the towering trees.

In this realm where humor is king,
A chortle, a chuckle, in everything.
From root to crown, let laughter confer,
In the jovial pines, joy will stir.

Banter Beneath the Boughs

Beneath the boughs, where whispers arise,
Laughter erupts 'neath the open skies.
Buds tease each other with gentle delight,
Tickling the air in the soft sunlight.

Digging through needles, a fox finds a hat,
A surprise awaits, oh, imagine that!
With every flourish, a punchline unfolds,
This woodland comedy never gets old.

The owls hoot wise, the rabbits share grins,
As the shy estuary begins to spin.
Each pebble giggles, each puddle sighs,
Echoing joy, where laughter flies.

Swaying limbs join in the play,
Filling the world with a cheerful array.
It's a festival here, a jubilant sound,
In nature’s embrace, joy knows no bound.

Smirks on the Slope

On the slope, where the wildflowers beam,
Smirks come alive in a sunny dream.
A juniper winks, what mischief it spurs,
Tickling the toes of the passing birds.

With every rustle, a punchline uncoils,
The laughter of critters, their playful spoils.
The breeze joins in with a ticklish sigh,
As secrets are whispered under the sky.

Mountains echo laughter, a sweet serenade,
While shadows play tricks in the late cascade.
Each pebble chuckles at the tales they’ve spun,
Living in joy, under the warming sun.

As twilight descends, the jokes don’t cease,
The world finds its rhythm, its laughter, its peace.
On this merry slope, where the jests are profound,
Every smirk has a story, waiting to be found.

Sassy Sprigs of Serenity

In the garden where whispers play,
Junipers giggle throughout the day.
They sway with glee, in the sun's warm light,
Sprouting punchlines, what a delightful sight!

Their needles prickle with joyful jest,
With each rustle, they invite a quest.
"Why did the pine lose at charades?
Because it couldn't leaf the stage!" they parade!

In the shade where laughter grows,
A sprig of sass in each jest bestows.
With spirits high and humor sprouted,
Nature's giggles, endlessly clouted!

So if you stroll where the junipers stand,
Prepare for chuckles, oh so unplanned.
For in their world of witty lee,
Sassy sprigs will set you free!

Radiant Radii of Humor

Sunlit leaves, a radiant crown,
Spreading laughter, never a frown.
With every sway, they tease the breeze,
Spinning tales that aim to please.

"Why couldn't the shrub find its mate?
It was too rooted to contemplate!"
Each quip rises from branches tall,
Wit like sunlight, embracing all.

Laughter dances in the forest green,
Where giggles echo and joy is seen.
With verdant humor, they all pool,
Majestic trees that bend the rule.

Amidst the grove, pure bliss prevails,
Radiant radii weave merry tales.
Join the jesters, the leaves so bright,
In nature's theater, pure delight!

Trees that Tell Tales

Among the branches and twisting roots,
Lies laughter wrapped in leafy boots.
Tales of mischief held in embrace,
Whispers of winter in a sunny space.

A squirrel once danced on a frisky limb,
To impress a bird—oh, what a whim!
"Why did he trip? It wasn't the tree,
He miscalculated his acorn spree!"

Like storytellers in a colorful play,
These trees will chuckle all through the day.
Branches lean in, as if to share,
Witty anecdotes that hang in the air.

So listen closely to the tales they weave,
Each laugh echoing, you might believe.
With sap and heart, they joyfully sing,
Trees that tell tales of everything!

The Lark Amongst the Leaves

A lively lark flits through the trees,
Tickling branches with whimsical breeze.
"Why do you sing?" the junipers jest,
"Because of the laughter, I feel so blessed!"

With chirpy notes, humor spills wide,
From leaf to leaf, where giggles abide.
"Why did the bird never wait in line?
It couldn't sit still; it's a feathered sign!"

Beneath the sky, the world high above,
Nature's comedians, showcasing love.
In every branch, there's a song to share,
With laughter ringing in the open air.

So when you hear that sweet melody,
Remember the jokes woven in the spree.
The lark amongst the leaves spins delight,
A harmonious dance, pure and bright!

Giggling Amongst the Foliage

In the shade where the branches sway,
A whisper tickles the leaves today.
The squirrels chuckle, the rabbits grin,
Nature's laughter hides within.

With every rustle, a punchline springs,
The flowers chuckle at small things.
Breezes carry a teasing cheer,
While mushrooms giggle, 'Oh dear, oh dear!'

Beneath the boughs, a jest takes flight,
As shadows dance in fading light.
The earth itself, a merry stage,
Where every doings gets a page!

So join the fun and take a seat,
Amongst the green, the laughter's sweet.
In every nook, there's humor found,
With giggles bouncing all around.

Puns of the Pine-Scented Breeze

As the pine scent wafts through the air,
Puns arise without a care.
A chipmunk grins and hops around,
With snickers echoing from the ground.

The breeze whispers its clever lines,
In rustling tones, the humor shines.
Branches bow as laughter sways,
Tickling toes in playful plays.

Each needle sharp, yet jokes so sweet,
With every gust, the quirks repeat.
A playful nudge from the canopy,
Reminding us to laugh, be free.

So let the wind bear your delight,
In every pun, the world feels bright.
Join in the fun, don't be shy,
Embrace the breeze as it laughs by.

Riddles Wrapped in Ribbons of Green

A riddle blooms beneath the vine,
With shades of green, they intertwine.
What has roots but can't be seen?
The answer hides where it's been!

Leaves flutter softly in quest for joy,
Each whisper a query, every twig a toy.
Nature's puzzles, a smirk in disguise,
As giggles erupt from the skies.

Within the thickets, secrets lay,
Playful enigmas brighten the day.
Beneath the ferns, a story waits,
As laughter bubbles and resonates.

So wander here, let your mind steep,
In laughter's embrace, where you can leap.
Each riddle wraps the air so bright,
With joyous laughter taking flight.

Laughter Layered in Leafy Shadows

Where shadows play, laughter glows,
With leafy smirks and nature's prose.
The branches sway with jests so grand,
As if the trees lend a helping hand.

In dappled light, the giggles pass,
A chorus sung by blades of grass.
Beneath the canopy, joy takes flight,
As every beam ignites the night.

Hush now, listen to whispers tease,
Life in the leaves, a playful breeze.
Where laughter nests in every glade,
And ne'er a frown or doubt is made.

So stroll through this patch of laughter vast,
Each moment bright, each giggle cast.
In leafy shadows, join the cheer,
For every joke is ringing here.

Wisecracks in the Wild

In the forest, laughter flows,
A squirrel tells jokes, everyone knows.
With acorns as props, they play their part,
Funny tails wagging, a true work of art.

The deer giggle softly, sharing a glance,
While owls on branches join in the dance.
A rabbit leaps high, a comic display,
Tickling the trees in a playful array.

Raccoons don masks, a daring disguise,
Their pranks bring forth chuckles and sighs.
With every rustle, a punchline revealed,
In this wild world, joy is concealed.

As the sun sets low, the laughter still grows,
Nature's comedians, the stars in their prose.
A symphony of giggles, in the fragrant air,
In the woods of wonder, humor lays bare.

Shady Shenanigans of the Cedar

Underneath the cedar, secrets abound,
Whispers of mischief are all around.
A crow cracks a joke, with caws so sincere,
Even the stones cannot help but cheer.

The iguana wears glasses, a wise little chap,
He's the punchline king, in this leafy map.
With each little snicker, the shadows grow light,
As laughter unravels the fabric of night.

The breeze carries giggles from twig to twig,
A dance of the branches, oh so big!
With each twist and turn, the humor takes flight,
Under the cedar, all's merry and bright.

As the sun dips low, the fun's far from done,
While critters and plants share glee like the sun.
In this vibrant life, shenanigans sprawl,
The cedar stands witness, to laughter's freefall.

Humorous Hums in the Habitat

In the thicket, a hum of delight,
Bees buzzing jokes from morning to night.
A ladybug chuckles, spots on her back,
Each tiny giggle a comedy track.

The hedgehogs wear ties for a fancy affair,
As fireflies flicker with luminous flair.
A cocktail of giggles in nature's lush chair,
Every shrub hums laughter, a joyous affair.

Amidst the tall grass, the shenanigans bloom,
A chorus of chuckles dispels any gloom.
The crickets compose, an ode to the fun,
While frogs on the sidelines cheer everyone.

As stars twinkle brightly, the laughter ignites,
In the warmbit of dusk, the humor invites.
Nature's own stand-up, with life’s warm embrace,
In this habitat rich, smiles take their place.

Mischief Among the Murmuring Leaves

The leaves are chuckling, a faint little tease,
As whispers of mischief dance in the breeze.
A lizard with flair steals a cookie or two,
With a wink and a nod, he devours anew.

The wind plays tricks, swishing hats off heads,
Setting loose giggles on the soft, grassy beds.
A daring raccoon hosts a show just for fun,
As the crowd of critters claps, all on the run.

With every rustle, the humor unfolds,
A tapestry woven of tales yet untold.
From branches they echo, the laughs intertwine,
In this quilt of mischief, joy is divine.

As the dusk settles down, the laughter takes flight,
In the backdrop of night, everything feels right.
Among trees and shadows, a comedy spree,
In the murmur of leaves, there's magic, you see.

The Cheer of the Conifer

In the grove where the trees sway,
Laughter echoes, come what may.
A squirrel trips on a hidden root,
And giggles rise, oh what a hoot!

Branches whisper, secrets shared,
With every rustle, humor bared.
The pinecones drop, a comical rain,
Nature's jesters, playing the game.

A woodpecker taps a silly beat,
While mischievous raccoons dance on their feet.
With each chuckle, joy takes flight,
In the conifer's heart, pure delight.

So gather round, let spirits soar,
In this cheerful realm, who could want more?
The air is filled with light and glee,
In the land of larks, wild and free.

Whimsical Woods of Wit

Amongst the trees where shadows play,
A jester stirs, come join the fray.
With leafy laughter that grows so bright,
Even the moon can't resist a bite!

Acorns fall with a plop and splat,
Scaring the fox and the chubby cat.
A giggling breeze tickles the ferns,
As nature spins its funny turns.

The owls wink, with knowing eyes,
As pine needles dance, a comical guise.
In every nook, a riddle hides,
Jovial whispers in leafy slides.

So frolic here, where humor blooms,
In this whimsical land where laughter looms.
Join the revels, let your heart cheer,
And find the jest, so wondrously near.

Forest Frolics Unveiled

Nestled deep in emerald shade,
A frolic unfolds, secrets laid.
Where chipmunks ponder their next big prank,
And every shadow has something to rank.

The rabbits hop with a zany flair,
While the trees chuckle, shaking their hair.
A leap and a bound, what fun it lends,
As laughter rings through the laughing bends.

The mischievous winds weave tales anew,
With each rustle, the sky turns blue.
Dancing leaves, in a playful race,
Nature's humor, a jubilant embrace.

So step inside this giddy retreat,
With every heart here skipping a beat.
Where whimsy reigns and spirits align,
In the forest's frolic, all is divine.

The Sylvan Smile

In woods where sunshine filters through,
A smile emerges, joyful and true.
The branches sway, a merry tune,
As shadows dazzle beneath the moon.

Beetles march with tiny hats,
While laughing trees sway, oh how they chat!
Whiskers twitch on the curious hare,
Wondering how to spread the rare air.

Each whisper holds a playful jest,
With whispers of nature, truly blessed.
From roots to crowns, the chuckles swell,
A symphony of giggles weaves its spell.

So find your joy in this glad parade,
In every creature, laughter is laid.
With heart aglow and spirits listed,
In sylvan realms, we're joyously twisted.

Amusing Accents of the Arboretum

In the garden of giggles, trees sway with glee,
Breezes whisper secrets, as funny as can be.
The blossoms share chuckles, sunbeams gleam bright,
Ticklish trunks tremble, in pure delight.

Squirrels with top hats, strut with flair,
While dancing daisies tease, without a care.
Each rustle a riddle, each shadow a grin,
Nature's own jesters, with laughter within.

Witty little robins, sing songs so bizarre,
Raccoons play pranks, under the evening star.
Branches bend low, with a cheeky surprise,
Every leaf is a punchline, under the skies.

With snickers and snorts, the forest takes flight,
In this playful paradise, everything feels right.
Joyful creatures gather, for a whimsical spree,
In this lively arboretum, you'll chuckle with me.

The Laughing Leaf

A leaf on the branch, giggles and sways,
Dancing with daylight, in mischievous ways.
Tales of the wind, twist and delight,
They circle around, like a feather in flight.

Old oaks share stories, of squirrels with style,
While acorns roll on, with a cheeky smile.
Nature's own laughter, echoing through,
Gleeful moments blossom, with every hue.

The sun winks down, as laughter takes root,
Every critter and creature, joins in the hoot.
Whimsical whispers, tickle the air,
In this very moment, joy's everywhere.

Through the branches and thickets, chuckles abound,
In the merry green patch, where fun can be found.
A tapestry woven, of joy and relief,
In the chorus of color, we find our belief.

Fables of Fun in the Forest

Beneath the green canopy, stories unfold,
Where pinecones conspire, and laughter is bold.
Mushrooms in capes, cast spells of delight,
Fables of folly echo through the night.

The wise old owl hoots, with a whimsical tone,
As playful shadows dance, never alone.
Crickets compose symphonies, under the moon,
While fireflies twinkle a mischievous tune.

A rabbit in slippers hops to the beat,
Making mischief with friends, oh what a treat.
Breezes are giggling, branches all sway,
In this forest of fables, let's laugh all day.

With every new tale, the laughter unwinds,
The humor of nature, so sweet it reminds.
In these woodland adventures, we find joy anew,
Where stories and giggles are woven right through.

Merriment Among the Moss

Among the plush green, where soft moss does grow,
Little creatures frolic, putting on a show.
Giggles of gnomes, echoing with cheer,
In this lush tapestry, laughter draws near.

Every tuft a throne, where fairies convene,
Telling tall tales, of the sights they have seen.
With splashes of color, and mischief galore,
Life's a grand jest, how could we want more?

Toadstools act coy, while fireflies tease,
Chasing the shadows, with grace and with ease.
Each moment a jest, the spirit runs free,
In this merry moss, find true jubilee.

With subtle chuckles, and smiles so wide,
Nature hosts parties, with joy as our guide.
So come, take a seat, and relish the rhyme,
In this haven of laughter, we're lost in good time.

The Gentle Jibe of Nature

In the breeze, the branches sway,
Whispering secrets, come what may.
A chuckle here, a giggle there,
Nature's humor fills the air.

Squirrels chase with frantic glee,
While wise old owls pretend to see.
The sun winks down with playful grace,
As shadows dance in a light-hearted race.

Blades of grass giggle as you pass,
Each step brings laughter, quite a blast.
Clouds above seem to jest and tease,
Painting smiles with every breeze.

Among the trees, tales twist and bend,
In every rustle, a punchline penned.
With every petal, a story's spun,
Nature's laughter, the sound of fun.

Juniper Jazz and Jest

Underneath the vibrant starlight,
Junipers sway, what a sight!
With twisting limbs of emerald hue,
They chuckle softly, just like you.

Whispers float on the moonlit tide,
As critters join in for the ride.
A raccoon strums a twig like a lute,
Making the night feel extra cute.

Breezes hum a jovial tune,
While shadows dance beneath the moon.
Junipers jig with every breeze,
Tickling noses like playful tease.

In the stillness, laughter spreads,
As chuckling critters share their threads.
Underneath the celestial jest,
Nature’s giggles never rest.

Tales Told Through Twisted Trunks

In the woods where the branches bend,
Trees shake hands, like a playful friend.
A squirrel drops acorns, a clumsy prize,
While the owls roll their eyes with surprise.

The pinecones giggle, they bounce and roll,
With every soft thud, they play their toll.
The wind tells tales, a tickling breeze,
Spinning stories with rustling leaves.

Beneath the bark, secrets collide,
Where laughter echoes, there's nothing to hide.
A frog sings loudly, his croak a cheer,
While the mushrooms dance, it's party time here.

The roots all chuckle, they wiggle and sway,
Telling stories of yesterdays play.
As shadows flicker, the fun won't cease,
In this funny forest, joy finds peace.

Jesting in the Juniper Shadows.

In juniper shade, where mischief plays,
A rabbit hops in the silliest ways.
The crickets chirp, a comedic band,
While the bumblebees juggle, quite unplanned.

The breeze whispers jokes in the rustling grass,
As the lizards slide by with a comical class.
The sunlight chuckles, tickling the ground,
While all of the blossoms sway all around.

Frogs hide in puddles, their laughter loud,
In this wild realm, they've gathered a crowd.
Each twisted branch holds a punchline clear,
And every tall tale brings a burst of cheer.

With giggles and snickers, the critters unite,
Creating a carnival, pure and bright.
In juniper shadows, joy's here to stay,
With laughter so rich, it lights up the day.

Whispers of the Witty Woods

In the woods where the wise trees cling,
A bat takes a nap while the chippy birds sing.
Each root and twig shares a tale or two,
Of pranks and escapes, of the old and the new.

The fox winks slyly, with a glint in her eyes,
While rabbits gather 'round, oh how time flies!
Every rustle and creak brings a chuckle bright,
As shadows dance under the silver moonlight.

The wise old owl gives a soft, wise hoot,
As the raccoon dons a brand-new suit.
Pinecones roll by with giggles galore,
Creating a ruckus, who could ask for more?

The river chuckles, flowing carefree,
With stories of laughter as far as can be.
In the witty woods, the joy's never thin,
With every soft whisper, the fun can begin.

Laughter Beneath the Canopy

Beneath the canopy, where sunlight spills,
The marigolds giggle and give hearty thrills.
The squirrels discuss their next sneaky plan,
While the hedgehogs chuckle at each silly man.

The petals all tremble, a ticklish affair,
As the butterflies' dance fills the warm air.
The tall trees sway, like they know the score,
While shadows of fun twist on the forest floor.

A snail makes a joke; it's slow but quite grand,
As the ladybugs laugh, they don't understand.
The dew drops twinkle, a glimmering cheer,
In the heart of the forest, laughter draws near.

Each creature can hear it, the giggles abound,
In a world full of joy, happiness found.
Beneath the canopy, the smiles unfurl,
Where laughter blooms bright in this magical whirl.

The Funnies of Forest Fantasy

In the woods where the whispers play,
A squirrel danced in a wobbly sway.
He cracked a nut with a humorous cheer,
And all the leaves laughed, having no fear.

The frogs joined in with a ribbit and croak,
Bouncing around like wild little folk.
They told silly tales of a turtle so bold,
Who wore a top hat and was a tad bit cold.

Under the moon, a wise owl would jest,
About humans who rarely know best.
With feathers ruffled in the shimmering night,
He winked at the stars, all twinkling bright.

So gather ‘round, let your giggles take flight,
In this forest of dreams, all merry and light.
For laughter’s the tune that the woods love to hum,
And nature herself can’t help but succumb.

Shadows with a Smile

In the shade where the shadows glide,
A raccoon played with a long, leafy slide.
He slipped and he laughed, with mischief in tow,
His buddy, the rabbit, hopped a bit slow.

The breeze tickled flowers, a whimsical tease,
As they swayed and danced with elegant ease.
A butterfly winked, affecting a spin,
While ants marched on, with a chuckle within.

Under a tree, a dragonfly spun,
Making up stories, oh what silly fun!
With every flutter, and every flap,
It painted the air with a giggly map.

From dusk until dawn, the laughter would bloom,
In shadows that whispered, dispelling the gloom.
For every critter and plant, filled with glee,
Knows humor's sweet magic, in nature’s decree.

Sprightly Humor in Sapling Stories

Amongst tiny trunks and fragrant green,
A baby tree shared a joke, unforeseen.
It wobbled and giggled, saying with flair,
"Why did they plant me? I swear it's not fair!"

The leaves below rustled, they couldn't resist,
They formed a chorus of laughter, a twist.
With every chuckle, the sunlight would break,
And dance on the branches, a vibrant quake.

A ladybug landed, so small yet so bold,
With tales of her travels, the stories retold.
"I flew over puddles, and slipped on a fry,
A burger was hiding, oh my, oh my!"

The saplings all cackled, their laughter so bright,
As shadows grew longer, embracing the night.
In a forest alive with whimsical might,
The humor of nature felt ever so right.

Giggle Grove Chronicles

In a grove where the sunbeams play peek-a-boo,
A chubby chipmunk shared jokes, oh so few.
He chuckled aloud at a fallen leaf's plight,
"How do you flip? Oh, what a great height!"

The owls joined in with a cackle and hoot,
Disguised in the dark, their feathers all mute.
They reminisced about their feathery pranks,
Spilling all secrets of floaty tree banks.

The bushes would quiver with every delight,
As laughter erupted and took to the night.
A gopher popped up with a grin so wide,
"I've buried my treasure, who'll come by my side?"

With every odd tale, and frolicsome jest,
The giggle grove bloomed, where humor was best.
For deep in the woods, where the whimsy unfolds,
A chronicle of laughter eternally holds.

Haywire in the Hollow

In a hollow quite wacky, the trees start to laugh,
A squirrel slips by, on a nut he will chaff.
The bunnies are giggling, with ears in a twist,
As the owls hoot jokes that can't be dismissed.

The creek bubbles over with stories so bright,
Fish wear little crowns, basking in moonlight.
A chipmunk performs, with his acorns all stacked,
The laughter erupts, as the whole forest clacked.

The breeze carries whispers, a ticklish delight,
Even the thorns start to chuckle at night.
Underneath the branches, where shadows reside,
A party of critters in mischief abide.

On branches, a jester flies high in the air,
All creatures are watching, their giggles to share.
With each funny tale spun under soft glow,
In this haywire hollow, the humor just flows.

Humor in the Horizon

The sun yawns awake, with a wink at the day,
While whispers of mirth chase the clouds far away.
A bear juggles berries, a sight to behold,
While the rabbits, all giggling, spin tales of old.

The shadows grow longer, the laughter runs wild,
As grasshoppers leap, in a dance so beguiled.
On hilltops, the crows play a game of charades,
While the daisies smirk in their green, leafy shades.

A fox spins a yarn, with a flick of his tail,
The logs aren't quite straight, but they sure tell a tale.
The sun sets ablaze in a tangerine hue,
A chorus of chuckles echoes out through the blue.

As night drapes the sky, with stars full of glee,
The owls share a cackle, not one bumblebee.
With humor in the horizon, all creatures align,
Under moonlit smiles, they toast with a vine.

Tales from the Timberline

Where branches do tangle, and stories are spun,
The critters unite, for the evening's begun.
A parrot recites every tale with a twist,
As the pines softly shake in a giggly fist.

The raccoons, they chuckle, with paws all a-fumble,
While the frogs croak along, in a swampy rumble.
A deer prances in, wearing flowers in hair,
With laughter like music drifting through the air.

The moon beams a grin as the tales intertwine,
With each whisker's twitch, there's a punchline divine.
The fireflies blink in a rhythmic parade,
As the night leads them on, to the jesters' charade.

In whispers of wind, the timberline sways,
With echoes of humor that brighten the days.
Each creature a part of this woodland delight,
In tales from the timberline, joy takes its flight.

Folly Amongst the Fir

In the grove of the firs, where the foolish do play,
A hedgehog in slippers prances round all day.
With jests and with jigs, the air’s filled with cheer,
As the acorns all giggle at absurdities near.

Wily foxes prance, in a comical race,
They trip on the roots with a clattering grace.
The owls tell their secrets, with giggles and hoots,
While the chipmunks prepare for their pun-filled disputes.

A nightingale sings of the folly so sweet,
As shadows of laughter flit ’neath dancing feet.
The grass sways like dancers, all joining the jest,
Amidst the tall firs, they all feel so blessed.

With each uproarious moment that dances in air,
Amongst the firs' laughter, there's joy everywhere.
For folly is found in this forest so grand,
Where every little creature gives humor a hand.

www.ingramcontent.com/pod-product-compliance
Lightning Source LLC
Chambersburg PA
CBHW051652160426
43209CB00004B/883
9781805673606